PROGRAM EVALUATION HANDBOOK

ROBERT C. SEROW

National Society for Experiential Education

SIMON & SCHUSTER CUSTOM PUBLISHING

Cover photo courtesy of PhotoDisc, Inc.

Printed in the United States of America

10 9 8 7 6 5 4 3 2 1

Please visit our web site at www.sscp.com

ISBN 0–536–01053–6

BA 98032

SIMON & SCHUSTER CUSTOM PUBLISHING
160 Gould Street/Needham Heights, MA 02194
Simon & Schuster Education Group

CONTENTS

FOREWORD

We are living in a time when the call for accountability in education is intensifying at all levels. Policy makers, funders, community leaders, administrators, parents, and students want to know what's working, what's not working, and why. I would argue that teachers, faculty, and practitioners want to know this information as well, and perhaps even more intensely as they are the ones charged with the management of these educational programs on a daily basis. Their need to understand what features of their programs are either contributing or not contributing to the development of stated outcomes is paramount.

NSEE offers *Program Evaluation Handbook* as a tool to assist stakeholders in the educational enterprise in better assessing the effectiveness of experiential education programs. This publication in many ways reflects core components of NSEE's strategic plan, namely:

- the importance of recognizing the common ground which all forms of experiential education share (*Program Evaluation* explains the major stages of evaluation for any experience-based program),

- the need for the development of standards to ensure high quality and promote best practices (*Program Evaluation* enumerates and explains the critical ingredients for an effective evaluation process), and

- the enhancement of the professional development of experiential educators (*Program Evaluation* equips faculty and program coordinators with essential information and expertise).

Program evaluation is, ultimately, a tool for ongoing learning. It is my pleasure to recommend *Program Evaluation Handbook* for use by anyone who is committed to thoughtful and well-executed experiential education programs.

Sally Migliore
Executive Director
National Society for Experiential Education

PREFACE

Over the past quarter-century, experiential education has attracted considerable interest among educators at both the secondary and postsecondary levels. As the field has grown in strength and visibility, so too have the possibilities for obtaining financial support from sources external to the host school or college. To insure that programs actually carry out the terms of their proposals, the funding agencies often require that an evaluation be conducted by a qualified specialist or, at a minimum, that the program maintain careful records regarding the delivery of services and the achievement of results. Of course, not all evaluations are implemented in response to funders' demands. In some cases, program managers or institutional officials are simply interested in finding out how well a program is working and whether it can be made to operate even more effectively.

As a way of acquainting experiential educators with the basic elements of evaluation practice, this *Program Evaluation Handbook* is presented in two parts. Part One consists of an introduction and three additional chapters that spell out in succession the major stages of an evaluation: planning, data collection, and follow-up. In each instance, the chapter provides overviews, definitions, and other substantive content, supplemented by examples and scenarios based on the experiences of educators at "Fallsboro College" and "Great Northern High School," two institutions that will not be found in any directory but which nevertheless seem to share the problems of real-world educational settings.

In Part Two, the *Handbook* turns to case studies at actual institutions. These cases have been contributed by educators from a variety of disciplines and are intended to highlight some of the many possible approaches to the evaluation of experiential programs. Each of the five cases is followed by a series of questions prepared by the editor. The purpose of these questions is to help readers make connections between the theories and guidelines in Part One of the *Handbook* and the issues addressed in each case. The contributions of each of the case-study authors are gratefully acknowledged.

Part One

AN OVERVIEW OF
PROGRAM EVALUATION

Chapter One

INTRODUCTION

This book is intended to offer experiential educators and other interested parties a brief, simple, and clear introduction to program evaluation. The underlying message is twofold. First, there is no single best approach to evaluation; rather, the most successful evaluations are often those that match their methods to the needs of particular programs. Adaptability, in turn, stems from necessity. Faced with tight budgets and impending deadlines, evaluators seldom can afford the luxury of holding out for one technique when something simpler or less expensive is available. Second, despite the need for flexibility, there are certain concepts now recognized as fundamental to the practice of evaluation. Although these core ideas are few in number and relatively simple to grasp, they are quite useful in identifying the type of evaluation that might be called for in a given situation.

The examples and case studies that will be used throughout this volume are drawn from the field of experiential education. Although educators working in other areas should have little difficulty in applying these materials to their own specialties, experiential education may be a particularly apt vehicle for acquainting readers with the fundamentals of evaluation. By their very nature, internships, practica, service-learning, and other forms of experiential education require that programs be adapted to the interests of the student. Yet it is this same flexibility in approach that sometimes makes it difficult to find a common benchmark for comparing one program with another—a step taken not only by evaluators but also by the external funders to whom educators often look for support. Thus, it should be recognized that evaluation involves not only the collection of data but also the management of relationships with *stakeholders* —that is, those individuals and groups that have an interest in the program and its outcomes.

Before proceeding any further, a number of issues having to do with background and context demand attention. Foremost of these is the necessity of defining our topic and distinguishing program evaluation from related forms of activity.

DEFINITIONS

The term "evaluation" is widely used to refer to the process of making judgments about quality or merit. Most of the time, evaluations are done informally, as when we decide how much we've enjoyed a particular video or when we assess the strengths and weaknesses of a new restaurant. In this book, we are interested in the more formal or structured process of evaluation as it is undertaken by educational institutions. More precisely, the focus will be on *program evaluation,* as opposed to the related but distinct processes of *personnel evaluation*, which examines the occupational performances of individuals, and *product evaluation*, which provides information about the perceived quality of a manufactured good. Program evaluation has a more diffuse frame of reference than either of these in that it weighs the merits of a set of activities that has been implemented by an educational institution in order to achieve a given set of objectives. A quick scan of the program evaluation literature would reveal that evaluators have diverse conceptions about the nature of their field. Some are content to accept a very general definition which holds that evaluation consists of any effort to render judgment about program quality. Another widely accepted definition is that evaluation is the process of determining the extent to which a program has achieved its goals and objectives. Others prefer a more policy-oriented approach in which evaluation involves the collection of information for the purpose of making decisions about a program. From the perspective of this book, any or all of these definitions are acceptable. Thus, the degree to which an evaluation should arrive at general judgments about program quality, emphasize goal attainment, or seek to contribute to decision-making is best determined by the evaluators themselves.

Evaluation, Research, and Related Activities

Common to each of the above definitions is the idea that judgments about program performance are necessarily based on empirical evidence. Insofar as it is an activity that systematically collects information, evaluation can be considered a form of *research*. Indeed, graduate-level courses on educational evaluation often overlap with those that deal with educational research. Contrary to the common misconception that evaluation is simply a softer version of "real" research, educational evaluators typically learn the same sampling and statistical techniques or qualitative methods as do other investigators. Yet despite their common methodology, evaluation and research do differ along a number of dimensions. The most basic distinction is the goal that each type of study tries to achieve. Stated simply, research seeks to arrive at generalizable conclusions about a subject and, in so doing, to advance the existing state of knowledge. The commitment to searching for new knowledge thus shapes all aspects of a research study, including the choice of a specific topic or question, as well as the timing and methods. For evaluators, such broader knowledge might be considered desirable but not essential, for the main intent behind an evaluation is to obtain information about a particular program. Consequently, evaluation procedures tend to be influenced by the circumstances of the program under study. In other words, the generalizability of findings matters less than their potential utility.

Closely linked to the differing purposes of research and evaluation are the incentives for undertaking a particular study. Many educational research studies are wholly or partly funded by the researchers themselves, for the purpose of achieving a personal or professional goal, such as completing a masters or doctoral degree, earning tenure, or simply learning more about their subject. With some exceptions, significant amounts of external funding for educational research have become very difficult to obtain. The full costs of an evaluation, on the other hand, are almost always paid for by the institution that hosts the program, either directly or as part of a grant received from a government or private agency. An evaluation is considered *internal* when the host institution assigns its own staff members to conduct the study, and *external* when it (or the funder) engages an outside party for that purpose. In either case, the person or agency that sponsors the evaluation and to whom the evaluator reports is considered the evaluator's *client*. (The program, of course, has its own clientele, in the persons of those who receive its services.)

Another activity with which evaluation is associated is *assessment*. Indeed, the two terms are often used interchangeably. Some observers, however, prefer to maintain the slight distinction that assessment is pursued chiefly through the analysis of students' academic performance, while evaluation tends to measure a broader range of program outcomes. Whether or not this is still a valid distinction is uncertain, as assessment activities in recent years have broadened to include such non-academic measures as student exit interviews and alumni and employer surveys.

Both evaluation and assessment have been linked to the movement to achieve greater accountability in American education. As costs have risen and test scores fallen, policy-makers, the media, and the public at-large have demanded that educators not only accept direct responsibility for the results of their programs but also that they step up their productivity by importing such quality-control tactics as strategic planning, Total Quality Management (TQM), and Continual Quality Improvement (CQI) from the world of business and industry. Program evaluation has played a part in such initiatives by presenting a means of judging the relative merits of specific activities within the organization. Probably the best way to avoid confusion about the relationship among these practices is to think of TQM and its offshoots not as alternatives to evaluation but as management tools that seek to increase accountability in part through the mechanism of program evaluation.

Finally, there are instances when the evaluator may find it useful to examine the wider context in which an educational program is embedded. In such cases, a *policy analysis* may be called for. Here, the emphasis is less on program performance per se than on the extent to which the program contributes to the distribution of a social, political, or economic good. Although there is no fixed point at which program evaluation ends and policy analysis begins, studies of the latter type often are implemented on a wider scale and use analytic techniques designed for these larger data sets.

Case Study
DISTINGUISHING BETWEEN EVALUATION AND RESEARCH

Megan O'Brien is currently employed as director of experiential education at Fallsboro College, an independent liberal arts institution. Before accepting that position, she completed her doctorate in Educational Studies at a large state university. The topic of her dissertation was "The Relationship of Learning Style and Personal Competence among Students Participating in Field-Based Activities." Working with a sample of 350 undergraduate students from the university, Megan investigated the extent to which preferences for certain styles of learning were statistically associated with students' scores on standardized test across several academic and affective areas. In addition to advancing her own career prospects, Megan's intention was to shed some light on a question that had long been of interest to her and which was also considered a crucial issue in her field of study. She also developed two articles from her dissertation, both of which were subsequently published in educational research journals. Every now and again, Megan gets a phone call or letter from a graduate student who has come across her articles and wants her advice about how to proceed in initiating a similar study.

In her new job, Megan finds few opportunities to develop new research studies. Because her position is funded in part from foundation and government grants, she spends much of her time conducting or overseeing evaluation studies of experiential programs at the college. Rather than asking a general question about the relationship between two or more variables (as she did in her dissertation), Megan now wants to know how well a specific program is being implemented and whether it is achieving its objectives. Although studies of this type usually don't allow her to publish her findings, they do provide one satisfaction: By showing the Fallsboro College administration and the funding agency that a program is effective (or can be made effective with some changes), Megan believes that evaluation helps to improve the quality of education at her institution.

HISTORY

The suggestion has been made that evaluation is a response to public demands for increased accountability on the part of educational institutions. Actually, educators have used program evaluation throughout much of the 20th century as a way of comparing programs and, more generally, of determining the effectiveness of their own practices, including experiential education and other innovative approaches. In the 1930s, such works as the "Progressive Education Association's Eight-Year Study" and Learned and Wood's "Pennsylvania Study," both of which will be discussed in Chapter 2, had an enormous impact on educational practice and even today are considered landmarks of sound design by both researchers and evaluators. The modern era in educational evaluation began in the 1960s, when the enactment by Congress of President Johnson's Great Society legislative agenda resulted in massive new federal funding for schools and colleges. Some of the most important of these laws, notably the Elementary and Secondary Education Act of 1965, contained provisions for the evaluation of new programs, probably as a way of offsetting concerns about the expanded scale of the federal government's educational expenditures. Similar requirements were subsequently adopted by other branches of government and by private agencies as well, so that most externally funded programs today are mandated to conduct some form of evaluation.

One further consequence of these laws was to spur the development of program evaluation as a field of professional specialization. Evaluation contracts became the lifeblood of newly formed consulting organizations, while government agencies at both the federal and state levels formed their own evaluation units. Hoping to capitalize on the burgeoning market for qualified personnel, institutions of higher education began to offer graduate courses, and in a few cases, entire degree programs, that were built around the study of program evaluation. Professional associations, with their own journals and annual conferences, soon appeared, as did textbooks distributed by commercial publishing houses. The capstone of this process of professionalization was the release in 1981 of a set of standards for evaluation practice. These standards have gained wide recognition in the ensuing years, and will be discussed in more detail in Chapter 4 of this book.

THE EVALUATION PROCESS

To this point, evaluation has been described largely in terms of the collection of information about a particular program. And indeed, the data-gathering or investigative phase of an evaluation usually does occupy the bulk of an evaluator's time and effort. A more comprehensive picture of the evaluation process, however, would also include the preliminary steps that must be taken to insure the success of the overall evaluation, as well as a follow-up stage in which results, conclusions, and recommendations are disseminated to key stakeholders. In sum, the evaluation process can be thought of as a sequence of three stages: planning, data collection, and follow-up.

Stage 1: Planning

At the outset of the evaluation process, few evaluators can be expected to have adequate knowledge of the program that they'll be studying. This is true not only of the outside or third-party evaluator, but also of internal evaluators, who are more likely to be employed in an institution's research unit rather than in an academic department or program. The planning phase therefore consists of the evaluators' efforts to become familiar enough with the program to design and implement the study and to make the most appropriate use of the results. The key questions that the evaluator should be asking at this point have to do with the program's goals and objectives; its relationship to other policies and programs; its origins and recent history; and the identity of its stakeholders, including both its friends and, if appropriate, its enemies. Much of our discussion of the planning stage will occur in Chapter 2 of this book.

Stage 2: Data Collection

Regardless of the methods employed, data collection usually accounts for two-thirds to three-quarters of the cost of an evaluation. One reason that these expenses are so high is that evaluators typically must gather two distinct sets of information, corresponding to program operations and outcomes. In the former instance, it is essential to understand the program's overall configuration, its means of service delivery, and the number and nature of the clients served. With respect to outcomes, the evaluator may want to look at the degree to which program goals and objectives are being achieved, as well as other effects, however unintended, that might be attributable to the program. The means that evaluators can use to answer these questions will be examined in Chapter 3.

Stage 3: Follow-Up

One of the evaluator's foremost obligations is to provide information that is useful to those who have commissioned the study. As we will see later, the usefulness of an evaluation report depends on, among other things, the timeliness, accuracy, and comprehensiveness of its findings. This implies that evaluators bear responsibility for understanding what their clients want or need from the evaluation and for maintaining effective communication with clients and other information sources. A related issue is the extent to which evaluators are expected not just to report their conclusions but also to offer recommendations for the future status of the program. Although such matters should be negotiated prior to the signing of the contract, evaluators may find that initial understandings with a client acquire new meanings over the life span of the project. The ethical and human dimensions of the evaluation process will be the subject of Chapter 4.

CONCLUSION

Chapter 1 has taken the first steps toward introducing readers to the field of educational program evaluation. It has done so by defining evaluation and distinguishing it from research and other related activities, by outlining the recent trend toward the professionalization of program evaluation in the United States, and by describing evaluation as a process consisting of three stages: planning, data collection, and follow-up. The remaining chapters in Part One of this book will seek to flesh out these ideas in ways that will be relevant not only to readers who expect to conduct evaluations, but also to those who will be their clients.

Chapter Two

APPROACHES TO
PROGRAM EVALUATION

As a relatively new area of specialization, educational evaluation has adapted many of its basic ideas from other branches of behavioral science. As one noted authority has put it, "the amount of content that is genuinely unique to the conduct of educational evaluation is mighty skimpy" (Popham 17). There is, to be sure, a substantial scholarly literature available, most of which consists of models or frameworks that blend theoretical content with practical guidelines for conducting an evaluation. For the most part, these frameworks arose in the 1960s and 1970s from the efforts of a handful of social scientists, measurement specialists, and philosophers to conceptualize the newly emerging field of program evaluation. Consequently, these models reflect varying understandings as to aims and purposes, the nature of the evaluator's role, the scope of evaluation, the organization of tasks, and many other issues. Since that time, these classic statements have been supplemented by others that have introduced further considerations to be taken into account in the planning or conduct of evaluation. The bibliography at the end of this book identifies several excellent sources for these materials.

However instrumental these models have been in shaping specialists' thinking about evaluation, it is probably fair to suggest that relatively few of the evaluations conducted today adhere completely to any one framework. As stated in Chapter 1, evaluators tend to select procedures from different sources according to the needs of the moment. In effect, there is little brand loyalty among practicing evaluators. This is not to suggest that the major evaluation models can be safely ignored. On the contrary, there are a number of ideas that originated in the early theoretical writing that are now considered indispensable to the work of program evaluators. Chapter 2 will discuss these core concepts in terms of three basic approaches to evaluation: decision-oriented, goal- (or objectives-) oriented, and comparative.

DECISION-ORIENTED MODELS

Recall that of the three definitions of evaluation discussed at the beginning of this book, only one made explicit reference to the use of evaluative information for decision making. Accordingly, we may define decision-oriented models as those that have been developed primarily with that purpose in mind. Models of this type are an especially appropriate starting point for our discussion because they have contributed four of the most familiar concepts in evaluation practice: formative evaluation, summative evaluation, process evaluation, and product evaluation.

Formative and Summative Evaluation

The distinction between formative and summative evaluation was introduced several decades ago by Michael Scriven as a way of highlighting the different contributions that evaluation can make within the decision-making process. Whereas *formative evaluation* is intended to provide information for the improvement of an ongoing program, *summative evaluation* is undertaken for the purpose of deciding the fate of a program nearing the end of its funding cycle.

Formative and summative evaluation are best understood as distinct but complementary practices. Formative evaluators are likely to be brought in at or near the start of the program. By focusing closely on the various aspects of the program, they will be able to identify its strengths and weaknesses and feed this information, along with their recommendations, directly to program staff. Therefore, good communications between evaluation and program staff members, a clear and detailed understanding of program operations, and timely feedback are essential to a successful formative evaluation. For summative evaluators, the primary objective should be the accuracy and comprehensiveness of the data collected. Although evaluative data are seldom the only factor that determines whether a program will be renewed or terminated, the submission of incomplete or faulty evidence in such cases represents not only a technical error on the evaluator's part but also a serious ethical lapse. (See Chapter 4.)

Case Study
FORMATIVE AND SUMMATIVE EVALUATION

George Lee is a veteran social studies teacher at Great Northern High School, an institution located in one of the nation's largest cities. Although he will be eligible for retirement in a few years, the expenses associated with having two children in college at the same time have forced George to look for opportunities to augment his base salary. One role that George has taken on this year is service-learning coordinator—a position that involves both fundraising and assisting other faculty members in overseeing the academic aspects of students' community service activities and assignments. In that capacity, he has been working especially closely with Ernie Costa, a young departmental colleague whose hands-on approach to teaching social studies has sparked great enthusiasm for community-based projects among his 10th- and 11th-grade students.

Even though George and Ernie see eye-to-eye on most matters, they have been unable to agree on procedures for the program evaluation that a local foundation is requiring as a condition of continuing its support for the school's service-learning activities. After carefully listening to a consultant explain the varying aims and advantages associated with each approach, George has concluded that a summative evaluation is needed. In his words, "Our program is strong enough to withstand careful scrutiny. If we make all of our findings available, the funder will have no choice but to continue its support for us—and probably even increase our budget." Ernie, on the other hand, wants to use the evaluation as a means of identifying those aspects of his project that can be improved. "The foundation's information needs," he tells George, "are not as important as our obligation to provide the best possible programs for our students." The consultant has informed them that the budget and timelines are adequate for either approach, but that she wants to get started within the next couple of weeks. Their principal has given George and Ernie exactly three days to arrive at a decision.

Process and Product Evaluation

We have just seen that the formative-summative distinction springs largely from educators' need to put evaluative information to different uses. However, it also contributes the insight that evaluations must be attuned to the different stages through which educational programs routinely pass. The implications of the program life cycle for educational evaluation are further elaborated in Daniel Stufflebeam's CIPP model, an acronym for Context, Input, Process, and Product. These terms represent the four types of evaluation that may be undertaken with respect to a single program.

The ultimate purpose of the CIPP model is to enhance the role of evaluation in educational decision making. Accordingly, each type of evaluation is expected to contribute to a different set of decisions. For instance, context evaluations aim at making better decisions in the selection of program goals, while input evaluations are used to insure more efficient allocation of resources once goals have been identified. Although the CIPP model as a whole is among the best-known of the major evaluation frameworks, most of the attention that it has received over the years has centered on the remaining two components—process and product evaluations. In fact, these two terms are so widely recognized that they are often used without any reference to the original model. As described by Stufflebeam, process evaluations "provide periodic feedback to persons responsible for implementing plans and procedures" (137), while product evaluation "provides information for deciding to continue, terminate, modify, or refocus program activity" (138). These descriptions are, of course, virtually identical to the definitions of formative and summative evaluation that were given in the preceding section. But the growing popularity of these terms has resulted in a subtle shift in their meaning. In today's usage, *process evaluation* refers to any systematic effort to collect information and to render judgment about the program's characteristic activity. *Product evaluation,* on the other hand, is the systematic effort to collect information and to render judgment about program outcomes. (Particularly in higher education, the term *outcomes assessment* is often used in place of product evaluation.)

In contrast to Stufflebeam's original definitions, contemporary usage does not specify that the data gathered from process or product evaluations must be used in any particular way. Product evaluation in particular is now being widely used for the purpose of improving the educational process. A current example is the growing reliance by colleges and universities on exit interviews with graduating seniors. The content of these interviews usually includes the graduates' perceptions of the highlights and shortcomings of their educational experiences. Although the exit interview clearly falls under the rubric of outcomes assessment, data may be fed back to the academic departments in hopes that they will be used to strengthen undergraduate courses and curricula. And as the pressures for accountability continue to escalate, ever wider and more imaginative uses will probably be made of evaluative data.

GOALS AND OBJECTIVES

Formative and summative evaluation and the CIPP model are prime examples of efforts to structure educational program evaluation for the purpose of sound decision making. However, some analysts believe that decision-oriented models unnecessarily place evaluators in the subordinate role of experts-for-hire who carry out the technical work of collecting and interpreting data but who leave the decisions to others. One alternative has been to place more emphasis on the judgmental component of the evaluator's work. This approach is exemplified by various *goal-oriented* models of evaluation. The goal-oriented models can be subdivided into weak and strong varieties. In the weak version, evaluators base their activity around program goals that have already been determined by the client. Given these goals, the task of the evaluator is to decide whether adequate progress has been made toward their attainment. The stronger version assigns the evaluator an active part in the formulation of program goals. In this view, evaluators are knowledgeable enough about the program to play a meaningful role in identifying appropriate outcomes. Once the goals have been adopted by the institution, the evaluator devises a plan for gauging the extent to which they are being realized.

As the above paragraph implies, the fundamental idea behind the goal-oriented approach is that the planning, delivery, and evaluation of educational programs should proceed on the basis of the outcomes that the program is intended to achieve. These intended outcomes are of two types: goals and objectives. Although most people use these terms interchangeably, in the world of program evaluation, each has a distinct meaning. *Goals* are general statements of intended outcomes. They are the larger ends that a program is to achieve. *Objectives* are more specific statements of intended outcomes, and so are often thought of as targets that must be reached in order to attain the program goals. The goal of this book, for example, is to help readers learn more about program evaluation, specifically as it applies to experiential education. In order to reach that goal, the book addresses a number of more limited outcomes or objectives, such as providing overviews of the major evaluation models and methods. (See also the examples provided in the upcoming section, "Behavioral Objectives.")

Educational Goals

In education, the goals of a program usually have to do with intended changes in students' knowledge or skills. These can be derived from any number of sources, including the educational research literature; the structure and content of an academic subject; state, local, and federal laws; and institutional traditions. Perhaps the most important sources of educational goals are the identified needs of the students and of the surrounding communities. The formal process of identifying student and community needs is known as a *needs assessment*. A needs assessment can be carried out by means of surveys, open hearings, expert consultation, focus group interviews, or simply by examining existing records. At other times, educational goals develop through an informal dialogue among instructors, students, parents, and other interested parties. Indeed, some of the most far-reaching efforts to develop new educational goals have begun at the grass roots level. (One example would be the growth of the service-learning movement in the United States, which gradually emerged from countless small-scale efforts to find ways for high school and college students to play more active roles in their communities and, by so doing, to enhance their own personal and academic development. Although there is no one list of goals for service-learning that everyone would agree to, few would disagree that service-learning aims at a closer link between campus and community, and at the application of subject matter to real-world situations, than do more conventional approaches.)

Behavioral Objectives

Once goals are established, it is possible to formulate objectives. Typically, several objectives will be identified for each goal. One method is to formulate objectives in behavioral terms. According to Popham, a *behavioral objective* should have three components: the condition under which a specific behavior is to occur, the behavior itself, and the desired level of performance. To illustrate the meaning of these three terms, consider the following example.

Goal: *Students will have a clear understanding of their career goals and will be generally familiar with workplace roles and responsibilities.*

Behavioral objective: *As a condition for graduation, each student will earn a passing grade in a semester-long internship in an industry or profession of his/her own choosing.*

This objective supports the goal of promoting career and workplace awareness by stating in precise behavioral terms what each student is expected to accomplish. In this instance, the *condition* that stimulates the behavior is the imposition of a graduation requirement. The *behavior* is participation in a semester-long internship in a field chosen by the student. The desired *level of performance* is a passing grade.

Goal-Free Evaluation

Along with the decision-oriented models, goal- and objectives-based approaches to evaluation are part of the mainstream of educational program evaluation. One reason for their popularity is that they afford a relatively convenient method for clarifying the intended outcomes of a program. Although not everyone who uses behavioral objectives adheres to the three-part formula suggested by Popham, the overall strategy of stating intended objectives in precise, measurable form has become widely accepted. Even so, there has been criticism that dependence on goals and objectives can result in an overly rigid approach to evaluation. One objection has been that formal statements of intended outcomes sometimes function as mere rhetorical devices that reflect neither a program's purposes nor its consequences. At worst, an evaluator's dependence on stated goals and objectives can divert attention away from a program's most significant strengths and weaknesses.

One alternative to the objectives-based models is *goal-free evaluation* (Scriven), which, as its name suggests, allows the evaluator to proceed without reference to formally stated intentions for the program. Instead, the program is studied by means of needs assessments, observations, and other techniques. Among the strengths of the goal-free approach is its potential for revealing a program's side effects, that is, its unintended consequences, either positive or negative. Despite this advantage, goal-free evaluation has yet to displace the goal-based models. This is probably due in part to the increased public demand for accountability and, more particularly, to the rise of strategic planning as a preferred management tool among American educators. Asked to rationalize their expenditure of resources, educational officials have found it useful to be able to explain their programs in terms of clearly specified relationships among an institution's mission statement, its goals, and its objectives (Keller).

COMPARATIVE APPROACHES

Accountability pressures may also play a part in the renewed interest in comparing the relative performances of educational programs. State-by-state or college-by-college comparisons of mean scores on widely administered educational tests, such as the Scholastic Assessment Test (SAT) or the National Assessment for Educational Progress (NAEP), are popular subjects for media reporting and analysis; increasingly, the comparisons even filter down to the level of individual schools, grade levels, and college majors and degree programs.

Evaluators, of course, have been assessing comparative performance for many years. In a now-classic example of such an analysis, William Learned and Ben Wood administered an extensive battery of academic tests to Pennsylvania college, university, and high school students in the 1930s. Their methods allowed them to draw inferences not only about the strengths of the students as individuals but also about the programs in which they were enrolled. Similar comparisons were undertaken in the *Eight-Year Study* (Chamberlin, Chamberlin, Drought, and Scott), which explored achievement levels among students attending progressive and conventional schools. On a more general basis, comparisons between experimental and control groups, on academic tests and other measures, constitute the heart of the quantitative methods that have long dominated educational research and evaluation. (See Chapter 3 for a discussion of these methods.)

The Stake Model

Given this history, it is surprising that evaluation theorists have paid relatively scant attention to the mechanisms of program comparison. Their assumption may have been that such matters were best addressed in courses on research methods, which were (and are) a separate and distinct enterprise from program evaluation (see Chapter 1). One exception is Robert Stake's article, "The Countenance of Educational Evaluation," which meticulously lays out a scheme for making relative as well as absolute judgments about the value of educational programs. Stake suggests that whether comparing one program to another, or simply holding it up against an absolute norm, attention should be directed to three types of program components. The first of these is known as *antecedents*, which are characteristics of the program and its clientele prior to the start of operations. Included here are the background traits and prior achievements of students, the qualifications of instructors, and the quality and quantity of resources available to the program. The second basis for comparison is the *transactions*, i.e., the treatment or intervention that each program offers. In the case of educational institutions, the transactions usually center on the actual delivery of instruction. Examples of these transactions would be the amount of time spent in instruction, the amount of material covered, and the demonstrated skill of the teacher. The third component that can be compared across programs is the *outcomes*, which would be assessed through achievement tests and possibly through some affective measures as well.

The Stake model gains complexity from its suggestion that evaluators explore congruence and contingency relationships within each program. The concept of *congruence* refers to the match between intentions and actuality within each of the three program components. For example, evaluators might prefer Program A to Program B if they concluded that Program A actually enrolled the students for whom it was intended (congruence of antecedents), that its instruction was delivered as intended (congruence of transactions), and its desired learning outcomes were achieved (congruence of outcomes), and that no such relationships were observed within Program B. The second relationship to be studied is *contingency*, which in this case means a cause-and-effect relationship among program components. Stake recommends contingency analysis as a way of ensuring that a program's outcomes are being achieved through the intended means. In comparing two programs, higher ratings would be given to the one that had a demonstrable relationship between instructional coverage and gains in achievement test scores (i.e., contingency between transactions and outcomes). In this circumstance, contingency between antecedents and outcomes would be undesirable, as when pre-existing traits, such as socioeconomic status, are found to have a dominant influence on students' mastery of subject matter.

To summarize, the Stake model holds that programs can be compared on the basis of three key components (antecedents, transactions, and outcomes). The comparisons can be undertaken either by observing whether plans are implemented as intended in each of the three program components (congruence) or by determining whether results are achieved through the intended means (contingency).

Cost Analysis

Another basis on which educational programs can be compared is cost. Many evaluators approach cost analysis reluctantly, preferring to leave this issue to those with expertise in economics or finance. Yet there are valid reasons for including program costs in a comparative evaluation. Specifically, clients are afforded a much better basis for decision making if they know something of the *efficiency* of each program, or its results relative to its costs. This is not to suggest that evaluations must include full-blown cost-benefit studies, which do indeed require specialized skills. Fortunately, evaluators have at their disposal some simpler methods of cost analysis which can yield useful insights into the relative efficiency of educational programs.

Emil Haller has suggested that one of the evaluator's first tasks should be to consider the *relevance* of each cost, that is, the degree to which it contributes to the current and future operating expenses of the program. From this standpoint, it is not necessarily the total dollar amounts that matter most in judging two or more programs, but the manner in which the costs of each program are incurred. For instance, a program whose largest expenses have already been incurred would be a likelier candidate for renewal than a program that produces similar results but whose costs lie mostly in the near future.

Cost relevance can be illustrated by reference to four pairs of concepts. In each pair, the cost that is more relevant is listed first. Note, though, that a particular cost may be relevant by one set of criteria and irrelevant by another. (For examples of each cost, see the boxed table that follows the case study.)

Incremental vs. Sunk Costs. An *incremental* cost is a new or ongoing expense that must be included in the program budget. As such, it is more relevant than a *sunk* cost, which has been expended prior to the start of a program.

Variable vs. Fixed Costs. Variable costs, which rise as the program expands and fall as the program contracts, are considered more relevant to an evaluation than are *fixed* costs, which remain stable, irrespective of changes in the program.

Recurring vs. Non-Recurring Costs. Recurring costs are expenditures that are incurred periodically over the course of the program. A *non-recurring* cost is a one-time expenditure.

Internal and External Costs. Costs are *internal* when they must be paid out of the program's budget, and *external* when they are paid from other sources, such as gifts or grants earmarked for that purpose.

Case Study
COST RELEVANCE OF VOLUNTEER TUTORING AT FALLSBORO COLLEGE

Fallsboro College has decided to establish an after-hours tutoring program for middle-school pupils in the community. The program is scheduled to begin during the upcoming fall semester. It will be directed on a quarter-time basis by a Fallsboro College faculty member, who will receive training in a two-day workshop. The remainder of the tutoring program staff will consist of unpaid student volunteers. The program will be housed in a College classroom that is currently not utilized after 3 p.m.

A snack will be served each day that the program is in operation, and certificates will be awarded to those pupils who attend regularly. The costs of snacks, certificates, and the director's workshop tuition and travel expenses will be covered by a small grant from a local foundation.

Examples

Incremental cost: Heating, cooling, and lighting of the classroom after 3 p.m.
Sunk cost: Construction costs of the Fallsboro College classroom building

Variable cost: Snacks and certificates
Fixed cost: Director's salary

Recurring cost: Director's salary; snacks and certificates
Non-recurring cost: Director's workshop tuition and travel expenses

Internal cost: Director's salary; heating, cooling, and lighting
External cost: Snacks and certificates; director's workshop tuition and travel expenses

---

OTHER MODELS

The approaches reviewed in the preceding paragraphs do not represent the full range of options available to evaluators. Two alternative strategies that deserve mention are the expert and adversary models. Many readers are already aware of the "blue ribbon" or *expert* model, which is used by accrediting agencies in secondary and higher education. Involved here is a two-stage process, in which the candidate institution conducts a self-study prior to the arrival of a visiting team. After conducting an on-site review, the panel makes recommendations to the agency concerning the changes needed (if any) for the institution to receive full accreditation for the upcoming five- or 10-year period. Another familiar format is the *adversary* evaluation, which mimics courtroom proceedings in that it places evaluators on two opposing sides of a debate over the merits of a program. Thus, one team (equivalent in function to defense attorneys), would assemble evidence of service delivery or goal achievement, while the other would point to deficiencies in these and other areas of program performance. The principle here is that it is not only possible for teams of evaluators to arrive at varying conclusions, but that it is desirable that they do so, inasmuch as the competition between teams will lead them to collect a more extensive body of information than would otherwise be assembled.

CONCLUSION

The models and concepts introduced in this chapter should be considered in conjunction with the planning stage of an evaluation. The basic issue that they address is the purpose that will be served by an evaluation. If the aim is to provide information for decision making, then a formative or summative evaluation or one or more of the CIPP evaluations might be appropriate. For evaluators interested in determining the amount of progress that a program has made toward achieving its intended outcomes, the best choice would be a goal- or objectives-based approach. When the evaluator's responsibility is to make judgments about the relative merits of two or more programs, a comparative model such as that proposed by Stake or one that emphasizes cost analysis would be suitable. And, of course, there are many other models that have not been discussed which would fit into one of these categories, plus an equal or greater number that exemplify alternative approaches to evaluation. Reference to the coverage of these models in a full-length evaluation textbook should provide some indication as to their applicability in specific cases.

Having explored the purposes that evaluation can address, the next step is to consider how the data are to be collected. This will be the task of Chapter 3.

Chapter Three

DATA COLLECTION

The core activity of program evaluation is the collection of information about educational processes and outcomes, and no issue has provoked more debate among evaluators than the means by which that information is collected. The lines have been drawn most clearly around the use of quantitative versus qualitative methods. Although evaluation was once dominated by the quantitative paradigm, qualitative methods have steadily gained popularity.

Today, this controversy appears to have abated somewhat, at least to the extent that many observers are now recommending that evaluators become familiar with both methodologies. That is also the position taken in this book. As in other matters, the choice of qualitative or quantitative techniques should be a function of the situation at hand. Some questions are best dealt with through the statistical analysis of experimental or survey data; others may require the detailed qualitative information gained from interviews and observations.

Chapter 3 briefly highlights the major steps in implementing quantitative methods; it then examines some of the ways in which qualitative approaches differ from the quantitative paradigm. The chapter concludes by sketching some of the conditions that might favor the use of one method over the other.

QUANTITATIVE METHODS

The term *quantitative* applies to a fairly wide range of techniques for systematically gathering and analyzing information. The common element among these techniques is that each involves the use of statistics, and hence is subject to the assumptions that govern statistical analysis. A good textbook on educational research can acquaint readers with the basic information that evaluators will need to know in this area. Our present interest, however, is not with statistics per se but with the procedures that evaluators should follow in order to apply quantitative techniques to the analysis of their data. In the interests of clarity and convenience, these procedures are presented as a five-step sequence: formulating the hypotheses or questions that will guide the evaluation; designing the study; choosing the research instruments; developing the sample; and analyzing the data.

Formulating Hypotheses or Questions

Quantitative research characteristically entails the testing of *hypotheses*, which are propositions about the relationships between the objects being studied. Hypotheses are usually stated in somewhat formal language, either in null form ("there is no relationship between variable A and variable B") or in directional form ("group A will show higher test scores than group B"). While some evaluators accept these conventions, others believe that it is simpler and more straightforward to frame their efforts in terms of questions, rather than hypotheses. This causes attention to be directed to the program itself rather than to variables or groups within the program. To illustrate, consider a team designing an evaluation of the community tutoring program established by the fictitious Fallsboro College. (See Chapter 2 for details.) A few of the questions that the evaluators might want to ask would be:

"What effects, if any, has the program had on the tutors?"

"Does tutoring lead to improvements in the educational performances of the participating middle-school pupils?"

"How has the program influenced Fallsboro College's relationships with the nearby middle schools and other community institutions?"

Note that each of these questions is formulated in fairly general terms. Depending on the evaluation model that is being followed, the questions would be derived from program goals and objectives or from a needs assessment conducted in the college and participating schools. The evaluators would also want to hold conversations with other stakeholders, including the program director, some of the tutors and tutees, and representatives from the local foundation that covers some of the program's costs. Another crucial step would be to review the research literature on tutoring programs and possibly to consult with experts in this field. The important point is that the questions or hypotheses that guide the evaluation should focus on the program's purposes, while also leaving room for documenting any unintended consequences associated with the program.

Designing the Study

Research *design* involves selecting the basic approach to data collection that the study will follow. The choice of quantitative or qualitative methods (or of a combination thereof) represents the most fundamental design issue. But within each of these paradigms, there are numerous other questions to be resolved before the study can begin.

The strongest of the designs available to quantitatively oriented evaluators is *experimentation,* a technique in which a treatment is offered to one group and withheld from another. By randomly selecting the members of the experimental and control groups and by manipulating the treatment variable, the investigator has created a situation in which, in theory, any observed difference between the two groups is attributable to the treatment.

Unfortunately, few educational researchers or evaluators are able to implement true experiments. This is because the conditions required for the random selection of group members and for the administration or withholding of treatments raise formidable ethical and logistical difficulties. The practical alternative adopted by most evaluators is *quasi-experimentation,* a blanket term for any research design that incorporates some (but not all) of the experimental methodology. The key to quasi-experimental studies is that variation occurs naturally rather than through the manipulation of the investigator (Campbell and Stanley). For example, instead of administering a treatment, a researcher might find a variable on which students already differ and then hypothesize the types of outcomes that might follow from that difference. This type of *ex post facto* design (so named because the study is implemented after the variation has occurred) is especially popular among program evaluators looking for a way of assessing the impact of programs to which some students are exposed and others are not.

Choosing the Research Instruments

The term *research instruments* refers to data collection devices. In a quantitative study, the instruments are likely to include subject-knowledge tests and attitude surveys. The selection of instruments will depend, of course, on the questions that the evaluator intends to answer. When measuring familiar outcomes such as academic achievement, self-esteem, and career preference, there are a wide range of instruments available that have been developed by large companies or by individual researchers. If these are too expensive to purchase or if information is needed about a topic for which no off-the-shelf instruments are available, the logical step would be for evaluators to develop their own measurement devices. In either case, effort must be made to guarantee the technical quality of the instruments; of particular importance is that the instrument achieve acceptable levels of reliability (a measure of consistency of response) and validity (a measure of the appropriateness of content).

Instrument selection or development often poses a particular dilemma for experiential educators, who find the available tests to be inappropriate for their programs but lack the specialized training that would allow them to feel comfortable in constructing their own instruments. One type of resource that can provide solutions to such problems is a standard reference work on educational tests and measurements. Fortunately, a number of such works have been published in recent decades, including the current edition of the classic *Mental Measurement Yearbook,* which is updated every few years (Close and Impara). Keep in mind also that most colleges and universities have testing libraries or centers, which may be open to the public. (See the case study, "Getting Help When You Need It," in this chapter.)

Developing the Sample

Some educational programs are so large that it would be prohibitively expensive to administer evaluation instruments to every participant. *Sampling* offers a means by which a relatively small number of individuals can effectively represent the entire population of program participants. Among measurement specialists, the preferred approach is *random sampling,* which offers each member of the population an equal and independent chance of being selected. For reasons already mentioned, however, evaluators generally employ methods other than random sampling; in so doing, they bear the burden of demonstrating that their sample adequately represents the population under study. One means of doing so is to *stratify* the sample, so that the sample's profile accurately reflects the makeup of the program population on any variable deemed to be relevant to the program. For example, demographic characteristics such as gender, age, race or ethnicity, and socioeconomic status, as well as individuals' prior academic achievements, are often important in educational planning and thus may be taken into account when creating a sample through stratification or other means.

Beyond arranging for similarity between the sample and the population, evaluators using quasi-experimental designs must also aim at insuring the *equivalence* of the experimental and control groups. As a practical matter, this means that no significant difference should exist in the mean characteristics of each group. This would be true of the demographic background factors mentioned above, and, more particularly, of any variable that might be expected to influence the results of the study. Suppose, for instance, that you are evaluating a week-long residential summer camp intended to increase computer literacy among 10-year olds. All tuition was paid by the school district attended by the campers. Results show program participants gaining an average of 25% in their knowledge of computer fundamentals, while a control group of non-participants from the same school district posted an increase of only 2% during the same period. Your entirely understandable first reaction might be to attribute the greater gains of the campers to the effects of a week of hands-on computer exploration. But suppose that on closer examination of the school records, you found that the campers had significantly higher scores on a standardized achievement test in mathematics that had been administered at the close of the previous semester. Insofar as math background is likely to have some bearing on the acquisition of computer skills, you, the evaluator, have a problem.

There are several ways of dealing with such dilemmas. In this particular instance, you could statistically correct for the math score differences, so that the adjusted results on the computer literacy tests are more likely to reflect the true impact of the camp experience. More to the point, you could have avoided this problem at the start of the study by matching members of the experimental and control groups on the basis of prior math achievement and, of course, other potentially relevant variables as well. *Matching,* then, is the process of selecting group members in order to achieve equivalence between the experimental and control groups. As a tool for insuring equivalence of groups within a study, it is considered second only to random sampling.

Analyzing the Data

Once their tests and surveys have been administered, quantitative researchers and evaluators analyze the results by means of one or more statistical techniques. Although the number of available procedures is enormous, the ones most often used to analyze educational data fall into two major categories: causal comparative (analysis of variance and its derivatives) and correlational (including multiple regression and factor analysis). Because these techniques are governed by certain assumptions about the nature and quality of the data, some analysts rely instead on less restrictive non-parametric statistics, of which the chi-square test is probably the most familiar.

Regardless of the procedure used, the bottom line for most studies is determining whether a finding is statistically significant. Thus, knowing that the experimental group outscored the control group might not, by itself, mean very much unless we also discovered that the difference reached a pre-established level of significance. Usually, that level is expressed as $p < .05$, which means that the there is only a small probability (less than 5 in 100) that the relationship observed in the sample is different from that of the true relationship as it exists in the population. Whether or not a certain finding will achieve statistical significance depends not only on the magnitude of the observed relationship, but also on the size of the sample, the nature of the instruments, and the type of statistics used in the study. One alternative view is that too much emphasis has been placed on statistical significance and not enough on the practical significance of findings. The argument here is, in part, that because the criteria for achieving statistical significance are essentially arbitrary, the interpretation of results should be left to those most familiar with the programs from which the data are taken. Indeed, concerns of this sort have led many evaluators to abandon statistics altogether in favor of qualitative analysis.

Case Study
GETTING HELP WHEN YOU NEED IT

The last time we looked in on George Lee and Ernie Costa, the two social studies teachers were trying to decide between formative and summative approaches to the evaluation of the service-learning program at Great Northern High School (see Chapter 2). Eventually, they decided to go with a formative design, with an emphasis on immediate feedback of information for the purpose of program improvement. Of particular interest to both teachers was the more effective use of weekly reflection sessions as a means of promoting students' understanding of the citizens' role in local government.

Their next step was to start designing the evaluation itself. Some of what they wanted was obvious. The study would necessarily be small, focusing on the roughly 60 students who were participating in the service components of Ernie's social studies courses. Given the funder's insistence on a tight timeline, it would have to be conducted during the current school year. Most importantly, perhaps, costs would need to be low—a fact that ruled out hiring an outside evaluator to collect and analyze the data.

The solution that George and Ernie came up with was to do most of the evaluation themselves. When they raised that possibility at a departmental faculty meeting, several colleagues pointed to a built-in conflict of interest in attempting to carry out the roles of program manager and evaluator. Others asked whether either George or Ernie knew enough about educational measurement to design the tests that would be needed or to conduct the statistical analyses of the test results. Discouraged, the two teachers decided to ask for some free advice from the consultant who had previously helped them choose between formative and summative evaluation. The consultant, Dr. Megan O'Brien of Fallsboro College, suggested a division of labor that would get the job done, on time and at little cost. Specifically, she volunteered the services of her college's faculty/student seminar on community research. The idea was that George and Ernie would meet four or five times with the members of the seminar; for each meeting, the two teachers would prepare a list of questions they needed to have answered about design, instrumentation, or analysis. If good answers were not forthcoming at the meeting itself, the seminar members would turn the questions into a homework assignment for themselves, with results to be reported in two weeks. Also, all of the concerned parties could communicate by way of e-mail, as Megan had created a listserv that would allow for instantaneous contact among the participants. When Ernie expressed some amazement at the group's willingness to donate their time and talents, he was informed that Fallsboro College, like most of its counterparts in the private and public sectors of American higher education, was increasingly committed to public service. The problem was not that the College got too many requests for help, but that the public seldom realized that advice was there for the taking.

As it turned out, George and Ernie did most of the legwork for the evaluation themselves. But the help provided by the seminar members saved them countless hours of library time, and steered them away from some technical blunders that might have wrecked their study. Several students introduced them to the College's Testing Library (which, as they soon learned, was a standard feature on most postsecondary campuses); and a faculty member from the Math department acquainted them with an inexpensive statistical software package that would run on the personal computers at Great Northern High School. Finally, two honors students in Sociology offered to help interpret the data in exchange for the right to incorporate parts of the evaluation into their own senior theses. By the time the project was finished, George was making humorous references to a second career in program evaluation, while Ernie was mulling over an application for a new masters degree program that Fallsboro College was offering.

QUALITATIVE METHODS

Although qualitative research includes a number of different forms of analysis, it does not apply to all of the non-quantitative methods used in the social and behavioral sciences. For instance, philosophical and historical methods of research are sometimes used by educational evaluators but are usually not what is meant by qualitative analysis. Rather, that term usually applies to certain techniques derived from anthropology and kindred disciplines. A useful way of explaining what qualitative analysis is all about is to show how it differs from quantitative methodology. This is best accomplished by temporarily adopting the perspective of the qualitativists, and then stepping back to see how the differences might be reconciled.

Assumptions

Qualitative researchers have successfully focused attention on the many tacit assumptions of quantitative social science, notably its reliance on scientific method as the best possible basis for interpreting human behavior. In accepting physics, chemistry, and the other hard sciences as its model, quantitative social science implies that human actions can be explained by reference to certain generalizations that, though not necessarily as deterministic as the laws of natural science, are nonetheless broadly accurate and useful. As seen by the qualitative camp, therefore, the aim of quantitative social science is to explain and predict human behavior by discovering the underlying forces that exist beyond the control or even the awareness of most individuals. This stands in marked contrast to the core assumptions of qualitative analysts about their own work. In essence, they believe that people shape their own behavior through the meanings that they give to individual and group action; accordingly, the goal of qualitative research is not to explain or predict behavior but to understand it. This can only be accomplished by understanding how and why actions take on the meanings that they have.

Procedures

Once law-like generalizations about human behavior have been established, quantitative research seeks to apply them in concrete instances. The usual procedure is to conduct experiments or quasi-experiments, in which hypotheses are tested. Though one cannot achieve complete certainty, the elimination of competing hypotheses through rigorously controlled studies greatly increases the likelihood that the resulting explanation is correct.

Qualitative evaluators, for the most part, conduct case studies rather than experiments. A case is regarded as a concrete instance of some larger phenomenon that is the true subject of interest. Having adopted the goal of understanding their subject, qualitativists seek to immerse themselves in the environment—a process that is both time- and labor-intensive. The research process begins with a careful review of the relevant literature, from which a series of tentative questions may be formulated. It is assumed, however, that the most meaningful questions will become clear only after the fieldwork has been initiated. So there is considerable flexibility in preparing the research instruments.

Although those instruments may take a number of forms, qualitative researchers and evaluators have relied most heavily on interviews and observations. These methods are also used by quantitative analysts, though in different formats and for different purposes. Depending on the type of information desired, interviewing may be structured, semistructured, or unstructured. Highly *structured interviews* are surveys conducted in oral form. They are intended to elicit direct responses to relatively straightforward questions; for that reason, they tend to be popular with marketing researchers, political pollsters, and other quantitative analysts. At the opposite end of the spectrum are *unstructured interviews*. Here, the desired information is more diffuse and more subjective than in the structured interview; thus, questions are open-ended, and ample provision is made for the participants to pursue a line of discussion in as much depth as needed. *Semistructured interviews* occupy the middle ground; while they make use of prepared questions, they also provide for some degree of flexibility. They, together with unstructured interviews, are among the most valuable tools for gathering qualitative information. A similar pattern obtains with respect to observations, which can be used either to quantify behavior by measuring the frequency or duration of actions or, alternatively, to assemble qualitative profiles of a setting or condition. In some instances qualitative researchers find it helpful or necessary not simply to observe a site but to become active participants—in effect, temporary members of the community. The role of *participant observer* requires considerable skill, and raises important ethical questions about confidentiality of data and the need for disclosure to other participants.

The next step is to analyze the data. Because of the volume and scope of the information collected, qualitative researchers normally attach great importance to *data reduction*. Whether the data were collected through interviews, observations, or other means, such as the examination of documents, researchers begin to organize the information into categories and then to search for underlying patterns within or between the categories. These activities can be thought of as the counterparts to the quantitative evaluator's initial inspection of statistical findings. Here, the idea is to determine which relationships are of greatest importance and then to center the analysis around those phenomena.

One of the characteristic modes of reporting qualitative research is *thick description*. The intent behind thick description is to provide as much detail as possible about the case at hand and to reflect the perceptions of the major participants. Those who read the description should thus be provided with both an accurate picture of the context and an understanding of the meanings embedded in the situation.

Triangulation

The most common criticism of qualitative research is that it is overly subjective, relying almost entirely on the impressions and interpretations of the researcher, as opposed to the more precise measures used by quantitative analysts. The counter-argument raised by the qualitative camp is twofold. First, all research has some element of subjectivity. Even ostensibly objective, highly quantified psychometric scales reflect the preferences, habits, strengths, and weaknesses of the analysts who develop and use them. Second, qualitativists do have established protocols for assessing the soundness of their work. Perhaps the most important of these is *triangulation*, a process in which multiple types of data, collected from multiple sources, are used for cross-checking facts and judgments, and thus for establishing the veracity, completeness, and usefulness of findings and conclusions.

Triangulation can involve a variety of procedures. One useful step is to determine the reliability of an instrument by comparing the scores awarded by different observers present at the same time and place. It is also important to validate information by careful consideration of a range of different sources and, if necessary, to reformulate initial findings accordingly. To illustrate, consider the accompanying case, based once again on the community tutoring program at Fallsboro College.

Case Study
TRIANGULATION

Congratulations! You have been hired by Fallsboro College to conduct a qualitative evaluation of its tutoring program for middle-school pupils. One question that the client wants answered is whether the program has any discernible impact on the educational performances of the participating sixth- through eighth-graders. As the evaluation proceeds, interviews with the participants point to strong positive effects. Nearly all of the tutors say that the pupils who attend regularly have shown real improvement in the quality of their work—a judgment supported by most of the pupils themselves. Your next step would be to obtain additional information by speaking with parents and teachers. Let's assume that their reports are somewhat more ambivalent; in particular, they say that while the young people love going to Fallsboro College for their tutoring sessions, they aren't spending much additional time in their studies and haven't shown any real improvement in their grades. A quick check of the school records (undertaken with the parents' written permission and with the cooperation of the school district) shows that although the grades have indeed remained stable, school attendance among the program participants has improved noticeably. Suppose also that telephone interviews with the school counselors indicate that the overall attendance levels in the local middle schools is about the same as in previous years. At this point, you might begin to formulate a tentative conclusion that the tutoring program is producing more positive attitudes toward school and thus better attendance. You would want to substantiate this in follow-up interviews, while also continuing to monitor school attendance.

CHOOSING A METHOD

Because the qualitative and quantitative camps are divided on fundamentals as well as on procedures, a resolution of their differences should not be expected soon. What may be more significant, though, is the emerging consensus among evaluators that each method can and should be utilized as the situation demands. The question that arises therefore is, in what circumstances is one method to be preferred over the other? Although there are no firm guidelines, some consideration might be given to the following points.

1. *Program size and scope.* A rough rule of thumb is that size favors quantification. This is partly because qual-

itative studies are labor-intensive and thus are inordinately expensive to implement on a very large scale. On the other hand, some programs are so small as to preclude the use of many statistical techniques that require a minimum number of cases to produce meaningful results.

2. *Audience.* Choice of methods may be influenced by the audience for whom the evaluation report is intended. Because their methods bring qualitative researchers into close contact with program staff, their reports tend to be utilization-focused—that is, oriented toward day-to-day educational practice. Conversely, quantitative methods aim at generalizable findings and therefore may be more useful for shaping policy decisions.

3. *Goals.* Quantitative evaluations work best when program goals are "precise, explicit, and predetermined, and (when) relevant variables can be identified in advance and validly measured" (House 17). Qualitative methods are better suited to programs whose goals are diffuse, changing, or open-ended.

4. *The evaluator's interests and skills.* Ideally, all evaluators will be equally adept at employing qualitative and quantitative methods. In fact, however, such is not always the case and some observers such as Rossi believe that the client is not well served when evaluators attempt to apply unfamiliar techniques. This quite naturally leads to the suggestion that evaluators work in teams so that all relevant modes of research and analysis are available.

Conclusion

The focus of Chapter 3 has been on data collection, the second stage of the evaluation process. Much of the technical work of the evaluation is performed in formulating the questions or hypotheses that will guide the study, in developing the research instruments, in choosing an appropriate design, in preparing a sample, and in analyzing the data. For some evaluators, the key decision will be whether to apply qualitative or quantitative methods. The strategy recommended in this book is to allow the choice of methods to be determined by such specific considerations as program size and scope, the intended audience, the goals addressed by the program, as well as the evaluator's own skills and interests.

With the conclusion of the data collection activities, the focus of the evaluation shifts to the third, or follow-up, stage. Here, evaluators often find themselves in the position of having to decide how they can best accommodate the interests of their clients in a manner consistent with their own professional and ethical responsibilities.

Chapter Four

Follow-Up

The familiar saying that knowledge is power seems especially applicable to program evaluation. By virtue of their access to multiple sources of information about an organization, evaluators can unknowingly generate doubt and fear among clients, who may worry that negative findings will destroy a program and undo years of their own hard work. Yet evaluators seldom see themselves as occupying a powerful position relative to their clients. It is the client, after all, who can hire and fire the evaluator, accept or reject the report, and add to or detract from the evaluator's professional reputation.

In response to such concerns, professional organizations have sought to clarify both the rights and the responsibilities of evaluators. As we shall see in this chapter, there now exist standards that have been developed for the purpose of guiding the professional behaviors of evaluators. First, however, let's consider several evaluation scenarios from the world of experiential education in which questions of power and responsibility loom large.

THE CASE OF THE SHRINKING CONTRACT

You are conducting an evaluation of a $5 million, four-year program aimed at strengthening the field component of professional education in a health-related area. As your work progresses, you learn that the program's board of directors was initially reluctant to commission an external evaluation and eventually agreed to do so only under strong pressure from the funder, a large federal agency. At a meeting just prior to the release of your first-year report, several board members inform you that they would like you to accept an important change in the evaluation contract. Specifically, they are proposing that you agree to a series of three one-year contracts, each of which would take effect only upon the acceptance by the board of the previous year's report. It seems clear to you that the board's intent is use the second-, third-, and fourth-year contracts as leverage to influence your reports.

Case Study
MORE THAN HIS MONEY'S WORTH

Tony Barnes is nearing the end of his second year as director of his school district's work-study program. A few months ago, he commissioned a formative evaluation, to be performed by several faculty members from a nearby university who were recommended to Tony as aggressive but fair evaluators. Although the price was a little higher than what Tony had in mind, the evaluators assured him that he'd be getting more than his money's worth. As it happens, that was an understatement. In the course of interviewing several student participants, the evaluators found out that one instructor expected her students to donate several hours every weekend to some projects for a small business venture that she operates on the side. When Tony read this in the interim evaluation report, he immediately asked the evaluators to delete the information about the instructor until he could inform his superiors. The evaluators are refusing to do so, citing their professional responsibilities as well as their obligations as citizens and taxpayers.

Note the similarities and differences between the two situations. The triggering event in each scenario is the impending release of an interim evaluation report. The focal points are also the same: the client's efforts to control the content of the current or future reports. A significant difference between the two cases is that the first is told from the perspective of the evaluator, while the second is viewed through the eyes of the client.

Successful resolution of the first situation may depend on the evaluator's political skills, such as discerning alliances and rivalries among board members or the level of support for the existing contract, and the ability to bring the influence of other stakeholders into play. Depending on how the existing contract is written, it might also be possible to ask the courts to intervene. However, given the time and expense involved, as well as the potential harm to one's standing among future clients, evaluators are understandably reluctant to pursue legal remedies.

The questions raised by the second scenario fall mainly under the rubric of client-evaluator communications. Foremost among these is the confidentiality or "ownership" of findings. This can involve not only the larger question of intellectual property rights, but also, as in this case, the ethical (and legal) responsibilities of the evaluator to report wrongdoing, as well as the timing and medium of the evaluator's reports. Ideally, such matters would be subject to negotiation prior to the signing of the evaluation contract. In reality, though, questions arise in the course of many evaluations that could not reasonably have been foreseen. Accordingly, some level of flexibility and mutual accommodation between client and evaluator is desirable.

STANDARDS

Like their counterparts in other fields, evaluators have a significant stake in the development and application of clear guidelines for professional practice. In law, medicine, and elsewhere, standards are codified in ways that are widely recognized not only by the practitioners themselves, but also by the courts and other regulatory bodies and by the general public. The origins of these codes lie in the acknowledgment that professional practice must be built on trust and that trust can only be insured when clear norms exist to guide the practitioner.

During the 1980s, 15 leading organizations in education and the human services joined together for the purpose of promulgating standards for the practice of program evaluation. The most recent result of their efforts is a list of 30 standards, which are divided into four categories: Utility, Feasibility, Propriety, and Accuracy. (See Table 4.1). The Program Evaluation Standards (as they are known) are intended as "guiding principles, not mechanical rules. They contain cautions and warnings against potential mistakes, identify practices generally agreed to be acceptable or unacceptable, and propose guidelines reflecting best current practice" (Sanders 8). As such, they provide a benchmark for experienced practitioners and a useful tool in the education of the next generation of evaluators. Yet they have not been universally adopted by evaluators, much less accepted by the courts or by the leading clients, such as the federal government, which has its own guidelines for evaluation. Likewise, the American Evaluation Association, one of the co-sponsors of the Program Evaluation Standards, has recently issued the Guiding Principles for Evaluators, a compendium of suggestions that in some ways duplicates and in other ways extends the Standards.

Taken together, the Standards and Guidelines illustrate the ongoing effort to establish clear criteria for sound and ethical practice for program evaluation. These principles may be of value as readers confront some of the dilemmas posed by the case studies in Part Two of this book and, more generally, as they come to terms with the intricacies of program evaluation in the real world of experiential education.

Table 4.1: The Program Evaluation Standards

Utility
The utility standards are intended to insure that an evaluation will serve the information needs of intended users.

U1 Stakeholder Identification
Persons involved in or affected by the evaluation should be identified, so that their needs can be addressed.

U2 Evaluator Credibility
The persons conducting the evaluation should be both trustworthy and competent to perform the evaluation, so that the evaluation findings achieve maximum credibility and acceptance.

U3 Information Scope and Selection
Information collected should be broadly selected to address pertinent questions about the program and be responsive to the needs and interests of clients and other specified stakeholders.

U4 Values Identification
The perspectives, procedures, and rationale used to interpret the findings should be carefully described, so that the bases for value judgments are clear.

U5 Report Clarity
Evaluation reports should clearly describe the program being evaluated, including its context, and the purposes, procedures,

and findings of the evaluation, so that essential information is provided and easily understood.

U6 Report Timeliness and Dissemination
Significant interim findings and evaluation reports should be disseminated to intended users, so that they can be used in a timely fashion.

U7 Evaluation Impact
Evaluations should be planned, conducted, and reported in ways that encourage follow-through by stakeholders, so that the likelihood that evaluation will be used is increased.

Feasibility
The feasibility standards are intended to ensure that an evaluation will be realistic, prudent, diplomatic, and frugal.

F1 Practical Procedures
The evaluation procedures should be practical, to keep disruption to a minimum while needed information is obtained.

F2 Political Viability
The evaluation should be planned and conducted with anticipation of the different positions of various interest groups, so that their cooperation may be obtained, and so that possible attempts by any of these groups to curtail evaluation operations or to bias or misapply the results can be averted or counteracted.

F3 Cost Effectiveness
The evaluation should be efficient and produce information of sufficient value, so that the resources expended can be justified.

Propriety
The propriety standards are intended to ensure that an evaluation will be conducted legally, ethically, and with due regard for the welfare of those involved in the evaluation, as well as those affected by its results.

P1 Service Orientation
Evaluations should be designed to assist organizations to address and effectively serve the needs of the full range of targeted participants.

P2 Formal Agreements
Obligations of the formal parties to an evaluation (what is to be done, how, by whom, when) should be agreed to in writing, so

that these parties are obligated to adhere to all conditions of the agreement or formally to renegotiate it.

P3 Rights of Human Subjects
Evaluations should be designed and conducted to respect and protect the rights and welfare of human subjects.

P4 Human Interactions
Evaluators should respect human dignity and worth in their interactions with other persons associated with an evaluation, so that participants are not threatened or harmed.

P5 Complete and Fair Assessment
The evaluation should be complete and fair in its examination and recording of strengths and weaknesses of the program being evaluated, so that strengths can be built upon and problem areas addressed.

P6 Disclosure of Findings
The formal parties to an evaluation should ensure that the full set of evaluation findings along with pertinent limitations are made accessible to the persons affected by the evaluation, and any others with expressed legal rights to receive the results.

P7 Conflict of Interest
Conflict of interest should be dealt with openly and honestly, so that it does not compromise the evaluation processes and results.

P8 Fiscal Responsibility
The evaluator's allocation and expenditure of resources should reflect sound accountability procedures and otherwise be prudent and ethically responsible, so that expenditures are accounted for and appropriate.

Accuracy
The accuracy standards are intended to ensure than an evaluation will reveal and convey technically adequate information about the features that determine worth or merit of the program being evaluated.

A1 Program Documentation
The program being evaluated should be described and documented clearly and accurately, so that the program is clearly identified.

A2 Context Analysis

The context in which the program exists should be examined in enough detail, so that its likely influences on the program can be identified.

A3 Described Purposes and Procedures

The purposes and procedures of the evaluation should be monitored and described in enough detail, so that they can be identified and assessed.

A4 Defensible Information Sources

The sources of information used in a program evaluation should be described in enough detail, so that the adequacy of the information can be assessed.

A5 Valid Information

The information gathering procedures should be chosen or developed and then implemented so that they will assure that the information arrived at is valid for the intended use.

A6 Reliable Information

The information gathering procedures should be chosen or developed and then implemented so that they will assure that the information obtained is sufficiently reliable for the intended use.

A7 Systematic Information

The information collected, processed, and reported in an evaluation should be systematically reviewed and any errors found should be corrected.

A8 Analysis of Quantitative Information

Quantitative information in an evaluation should be appropriately and systematically analyzed so that evaluation questions are effectively answered.

A9 Analysis of Qualitative Information

Qualitative information in an evaluation should be appropriately and systematically analyzed so that evaluation questions are effectively answered.

A10 Justified Conclusions

The conclusions reached in an evaluation should be explicitly justified, so that stakeholders can assess them.

A11 Impartial Reporting

Reporting procedures should guard against distortion caused by personal feelings and biases of any party to the evaluation, so that evaluation reports fairly reflect the evaluation findings.

A12 Meta-Evaluation

The evaluation itself should be formatively and summatively evaluated against these and other pertinent standards, so that its conduct is appropriately guided and, on completion, stakeholders can closely examine its strengths and weaknesses.

Source: Sanders, 1994.

CONCLUSION

With this discussion of the follow-up stage, we have now completed our overview of the evaluation process. To reiterate an earlier point, those interested in obtaining additional information should review the materials listed in the bibliography at the end of this book. Yet, program evaluation has always been a practitioner-oriented field, in which theoretical models and other scholarly ideas have drawn less attention than the concrete problems that emerge from the daily experience of the evaluator. The next step for us, therefore, will be to examine a series of case studies pertaining to the evaluation of experiential programs at institutions of higher education. Although the contributing authors approach the evaluation process from a variety of perspectives (such as liberal arts or preprofessional studies, faculty or administration, large university or small college), each of the five cases highlights one or more of the practical issues that evaluators confront in the course of their work.

Part Two

Case Studies

Case #1
EVALUATING SERVICE-LEARNING

Beth Olsen and Helen Reilly
The Richard Stockton College of New Jersey

The Richard Stockton College of New Jersey is a public, four-year undergraduate liberal arts college with a current enrollment of 4,732 students. Its current Carnegie classification is Baccalaureate I.

We first began service-learning (SL) in 1991 with a grant from the state and participation by two faculty members. Since then, our numbers have grown to include 19 faculty members teaching 27 course sections to about 350 students annually. The number of community partners has grown to include 100 mostly nonprofit agencies who define their own needs and request SL students to help meet those needs. During this time, we have laid foundations to support service-learning: an infrastructure of forms and procedures has been put in place, coordinated by staff members in Academic Affairs.

Having done this much, we felt that it was time for reflection. As part of an evaluation, we sent surveys to our community partners and to faculty members teaching service-learning classes. For purposes of comparison, surveys were also sent to some faculty members not involved with SL. In addition, we have administered pre- and post-tests to our students as a way of gauging their perceptions and learning outcomes from the service-learning experience and of assessing such psychological orientations as empathy and ethnocentrism. We have also collected qualitative data from students who have participated in service-learning. This information is gleaned from students' journals and from focused interviews with faculty and agency staff. Finally, to gain another perspective on our process, we will be hiring a consultant to give us an outsider's view of what we do and how we do it.

The evaluation process is influenced by two features that have defined our program from the beginning. First, service-learning at Stockton is resolutely grounded in academics, with the SL experience understood primarily as a way of teaching and learning. Second, SL is also a means to provide students with cross-cultural experiences, and to afford them opportunities to interact with people of various gender, age, socio-economic, and ethnic characteristics.

Follow-Up Discussion to Case #1

In addition to conducting their own evaluation of service-learning, the authors state that they will be bringing in an outside consultant. What are some of the issues not addressed by the internal evaluation that the consultant might focus on? From the context of this case, would the outside evaluation be more likely to be formative or summative in nature? Why? What types of data would the consultant need to collect in order to address this purpose? How would those data differ from what has already been collected?

Case #2
AN EXPERIENTIAL LEARNING PROJECT
THAT MADE A DIFFERENCE

Linda Ferrell
Southeast Missouri State College

Retention has emerged as a major concern for universities and colleges experiencing declining enrollments. One such institution, Southeast Missouri State University, has initiated a project designed to identify students at risk of dropping out and to reduce the likelihood of their attrition by implementing an experiential learning project that addresses their scholastic concerns.

Data compiled by Southeast Missouri State University's Office of Institutional Research revealed a 21 percent attrition rate among majors in the Department of Criminal Justice. An analysis of the data alerted the department to certain identifiable retention problem areas. The most compelling problem was that a significant number of majors had failed the University's mandated 75-hour Writing Proficiency Exam. This group faced a substantial risk of attrition because only those who pass the examination may be considered as candidates for graduation.

Guided by research on the effectiveness of experiential education in promoting learning, the Department of Criminal Justice initiated an active learning project to advance the students' written communication skills.

PROGRAM GOALS

It was determined that students who performed poorly in their introductory English course were likely to experience difficulties in writing, which can directly affect test performance. Therefore, criminal justice majors who had failed the Writing Proficiency Exam and those who received a grade of D or below in EN 140 were included in the intervention program.

This program offers students an opportunity to develop strengths in written communication by applying their writing skills to an actual field experience. It also aims at raising students' awareness of the importance of written communication skills for criminal justice professionals, and to strengthen their commitment to successfully completing their college degree.

THE FIELD EXPERIENCE

Students were required to visit an agency where criminal justice professionals utilized written communication. Such settings included law enforcement departments, correctional facilities, probation and parole offices, juvenile offices, and youth centers.

Once a setting had been selected, the students made arrangements to observe the criminal justice professionals at work. There were no prescribed parameters guiding the breadth of the field experience. However, the students were expected to conduct interviews, keep notes, and compose a three-page essay on the importance of written communication skills in the selected setting.

The essays specifically described and explained the many ways in which writing skills were utilized by professionals in the selected setting. The essays culminated with a discussion of the impact of the field experience and how it added knowledge not obtained from criminal justice or English courses.

Students were assigned a writing consultant in the university's Writing Center to assist the students by analyzing the written essays. The analysis addressed various aspects of composition including using transitions to achieve coherence, writing introductions and conclusions, incorporating quoted material, and editing for clarity, development, and organization.

FINDINGS

Since its inception, 27 students have participated in the experiential learning program. Some have indicated that their active participation in the project has increased their awareness of the importance of written communication to criminal justice professionals. In the words of one student who assisted a probation officer for a week:

> The papers that I have to do for my academic classes never really showed how vital written communication can be. Without good writing skills, I would not be able to write a report that would stand up in court.

Another student, after observing a U.S. Marshal, went a step further in examining the importance of written communication in the field of criminal justice by remarking:

> I knew writing was important in any criminal justice field, but I was unaware of how it is essential. Writing affects everything you do on an everyday basis. It is one true reflection of your job performance, and you cannot perform your job if you cannot write.

Most of the students suggested that the experience had forced them to acknowledge a need to deal with their poor writing skills. One student reflected on how the active learning experience generated a stronger commitment to academic performances by stating:

> This experience has given me some knowledge where I am weakest and given me time to become better at strengthening those weaknesses.

Many students related that the project allowed them to become more actively involved in the field, reinforced their desire to obtain a college degree, and inspired them to continue to pursue a career in the criminal justice field. After visiting a local police department, one student remarked:

> I definitely know that this is what I want to do and I know now that I can do it. I'm glad I got to go talk to [the chief-of-police]. He let me read some reports. I couldn't believe how much writing a police officer does. He convinced me that I should stay in school and get a degree and made it very clear that I need to be a good writer. He said that the best thing I could do to help me find a job is to learn how to write.

IMPLICATIONS

The Department of Criminal Justice had experienced one of the larger failure rates among students taking the Writing Proficiency Exam. In academic years 1993–94 and 1994–95, the failure rates among criminal justice students were 28 and 33 percent, respectively. Following the implementation of this project, only 17 percent of all criminal justice students who took the Writing Proficiency Exam have failed. Of those students who have participated in this project, 100 percent have passed.

With respect to retention, only one (4 percent) of the participating students dropped out of school even though 20 (74 percent) students from this group had expressed that, prior to the project, they had considered dropping out.

CONCLUSIONS

The results of this study of the connection between an experiential learning project and student retention should be considered cautiously. Because they are not the product of a controlled experiment, a causal relationship can not be inferred. The findings are, however, consistent with literature suggesting that positive interactions among faculty, students, and the community promote learning. The project seemed to encourage the students to become actively involved in their education and the students overall experienced increases in their writing skills. The data suggest that this "student-centered" experiential learning project, which specifically addressed the needs of a targeted group, played a significant role in reducing the rate of attrition of our criminal justice majors.

Follow-Up Discussion to Case #2

The author warns that because the study was not conducted as a controlled experiment, its findings can be accepted only with caution. Yet the title and the concluding paragraph clearly suggest that the writing program has helped to reduce student attrition. As a reader, are you prepared to accept this conclusion? If so, what data presented in the case study do you find convincing? If not, what additional evidence what you like to see presented? To what extent would it be useful to have included qualitative data, such as student interviews, in the evaluation?

Case #3
THE LEARNING CONTRACT: A VEHICLE FOR INVOLVING STUDENTS IN EVALUATION

Jane Callahan and Ellen Salvatore
Providence College

This case study describes the evaluation component of a two-semester practicum course at Providence College that is required of students majoring in Public and Community Studies (PCS). The topics to be presented in the case study are the goals and structure of the practicum, the role of students in supporting service-learning courses, and, in particular, the use of learning contracts and portfolios as a means of evaluating students' accomplishments.

GOALS AND STRUCTURE OF THE PRACTICUM

The Public and Community Studies major was developed as part of an endowment aimed at promoting service and service-learning at Providence College. In order to help students develop the knowledge and skills needed to coordinate community service activities and to support faculty members teaching classes with an SL component, all PCS majors are required to serve as teaching assistants (TAs) in such courses. The TAs' responsibilities include providing orientation to other students at service sites, coordinating and scheduling service, and leading reflection sessions. At the same time, TAs strengthen their own understanding of community service and develop the skills necessary to work effectively in a variety of community roles.

The role of teaching assistant is at the heart of the practicum experience. Some of the specific goals addressed by the practicum are the development of leadership and communication skills, as well as decision making and problem solving. Students are encouraged to consider their own skill levels and to target those in which they would like to make changes. The practicum faculty, meanwhile, help students to apply the targeted skill areas to the practicum itself. For example, rather than providing solutions, students are encouraged to devise their own strategies for solving problems. One important component of the practicum is the seminar, which is identified as the place where TAs can freely discuss the problems encountered in their role as teaching assistants. More generally, the practicum is intended to foster a democratic community in which students feel free to share their concerns, frustrations, and accomplishments.

THE LEARNING CONTRACT

Evaluation is difficult in a course like this. Students are working in a variety of settings and although as many as four TAs may be assigned to a single service-learning course, each may have chosen to concentrate on the development of different skill areas. In order to allow for the individualization of outcomes, promote student ownership of learning, and encourage students' involvement in evaluation, the practicum faculty decided to employ student learning contracts. The two-part format of the learning contract used in the practicum is based on that developed by Margaret Roderick of the Department of Social Work at Providence College. First, it identifies the roles and responsibilities of the student, faculty member, and site supervisor; second, it specifies the individual student learning outcomes and describes how each will be evaluated.

The use of learning contracts has posed challenges for students and faculty alike. Most students are initially uncomfortable with the idea that they, rather than the practicum faculty, bear primary responsibility for identifying what they want to learn, how they will learn it, and how they will evaluate whether the intended learning has taken place. In order to provide a framework for developing the contract, guidelines and purpose statements are provided to students. After examining these materials, students are encouraged to meet with the SL course faculty to negotiate their responsibilities for site and class work. With assistance, students are able to examine the context of their learning over the semester and to consider the skills that they will need to fulfill their individual work assignments.

More problematic is each student's role in formulating and assessing learning objectives. There are three dimensions to this issue. First, students tend to focus more readily on what they will do (such as providing orientation at the service site) than on developing specific learning objectives for each activity (for example, strengthening one's communication skills). Second, they often have difficulty determining how to measure their success in attaining each objective. Written evaluations, surveys, and conferences are frequently used to obtain feedback, but unless the objectives are written in behavioral terms, students may not be able to conceive of an appropriate method of evaluation. One student, for instance, listed the following objective: "To learn freely and to give more than I take." Because global objectives such as this are nearly impossible to evaluate accurately, the practicum faculty work closely with individual students to develop intended learning outcomes that can be understood by all parties and subjected to relatively concrete forms of measurement. Third, and perhaps most important, many students are uncomfortable with the entire notion of evaluation. Because they are evaluating not only performance but personal development, and because they work hard and are very much invested in the work they do, students tend to interpret negative feedback as somehow devaluing their work and themselves. Related to this is that students are aware that it is more difficult to evaluate leadership, problem solving, and other general skills than to evaluate mastery of academic knowledge, as is the practice in most of their courses. These issues, when linked to the fact that the evaluation is considered part of the grading process, present students with a situation that many would rather avoid.

IMPLEMENTATION

At the end of each semester, students use the learning contracts to construct a written self-evaluation. Including feedback from their service-learning faculty, from their site supervisors, and from the students enrolled in their SL course, students analyze and document the extent to which they have fulfilled their responsibilities and met the objectives set forth in the contract. The self-evaluation, supplemented by supporting documents, photographs, videos, journals, and projects completed at the site, is then incorporated into a portfolio and submitted to the practicum faculty. These materials are then reviewed during a meeting between faculty members and the student. This conference allows for mutual feedback and for exchanging views about the learning experience and about the evaluation. It also produces a grade jointly determined by faculty members and the student.

IMPLICATIONS

Although students have initially resisted the use of learning contracts, faculty believe that the contracts have not only encouraged students to take responsibility for their own learning but also provide a suitable basis for evaluating the experiential learning process. By developing individual learning objectives, students tailor learning to meet their own needs. And by formulating measures for assessing the achievement of those objectives, each student plays a meaningful role in the evaluation process. The process has sometimes been a painful one for faculty as well as students, but results demonstrate that it has often been worth the time and effort invested. By the end of the second semester, the comments made by students usually indicate that the learning contract has helped them to focus on individual, measurable objectives and to evaluate whether the objectives have been met.

Follow-Up Discussion to Case #3

This case deals with the assessment of student outcomes in a service-learning practicum. Its unique feature is the very active role played by the students themselves in setting objectives, assessing performance levels, and awarding grades.

Compare this approach with a standard instructor-driven assessment. What are the advantages of each approach? Of the major evaluation models discussed in the first part of this book (decision-oriented, goal-oriented, and comparative), which most resembles the procedures described in this case study? What are the most important points of similarity? Other than those mentioned by the authors, what other types of information might a funder or campus decision maker want to have collected as part of an overall evaluation of the service-learning practicum?

Case #4
EVALUATING A WEB-BASED COURSE

Robert C. Serow, George R. Hess, Robert C. Abt, and Chinasa V. Ukpabi
North Carolina State University

North Carolina State University is classified as a Research I institution, and is known internationally for its programs in engineering, forestry, agriculture, and other applied science fields. In recent years, it has begun to develop the technological infrastructure for delivering educational programs across ever-increasing distances. One component of NC State's vision for distance education involves the extensive use of the Internet, and more precisely, the World Wide Web, as a delivery vehicle. The following case study describes an evaluation of a Web-based course that was conducted during the Fall of 1996. To preserve confidentiality, some details have been altered.

THE COURSE

ENV 991 (Issues in Ecology and Economics) was designed by members of the College of Environmental Studies as a highly experimental graduate course that was intended to blaze a new trail in the distance learning landscape. The instructors wanted to combine two established alternatives to traditional instruction—namely, interdisciplinary and experiential education—with Web-based communication technology. Using the Web as the primary means of communication, the participants (five or six students in several applied science programs at NC State and at a neighboring university) would be expected to systematically develop and explore ideas related to a current environmental issue and then to present these ideas to an informal symposium of peers, faculty members, and outside stakeholders. More concretely, the class would use the ENV 991 home page to set forth their own ideas, to comment on the thoughts posted by others, to recommend readings, and, in general, to do all of the things that a graduate-level course usually accomplishes in person. To emphasize the Web's pivotal role, the class was scheduled for only a handful of face-to-face meetings during the semester. Thus, the instructors of record expected to serve chiefly as facilitators of an electronically based process of individual and small-group learning, rather than to perform the traditional professorial role of disseminating an existing body of knowledge via weekly lectures and in-person seminars. In keeping with the experimental nature of the course, grading would be on a pass/fail basis.

THE EVALUATION

Recognizing that the success of one Web-based course might lead to others, and that a string of such successes would eventually free academic programs from many of the constraints customarily imposed by time and space, the Provost's Office at NC State agreed to underwrite the start-up costs of ENV 991 and to pay for a third-party evaluation. The evaluation team, consisting of a faculty member and a doctoral student in NC State's College of Education and Psychology, took this action to mean that beyond the specific issues associated with this one course, ENV 991 was regarded in some influential sectors of the university as a proving ground for future high-tech developments in program planning and course delivery. Accordingly, it seemed clear that a relatively open-ended formative approach to the evaluation was called for. The instructors, meanwhile, stated their interest in gaining information about the effectiveness of four aspects of the course: students' acquisition of knowledge and the formation of attitudes towards the environmental questions at issue; the self- and peer-oriented model of instruction; the interdisciplinary flavor of the course; and the reliance on the Web as a primary vehicle of instruction. (A fifth objective—the role of corporate and other external stakeholders—did not materialize as planned and was thus dropped from the evaluation).

Some thought was given to the possibility of conducting a high-tech evaluation by using the Web as the principal means of data collection. However, a variety of ethical and practical issues, having to do with the need to protect source confidentiality and to foster trust between the evaluators and other participants, resulted in a decision to go with a relatively conventional low-tech approach. More precisely, the desired information was obtained primarily through pre- and post-course focus groups conducted with the students and through interviews with the two instructors, also conducted at the beginning and end of the semester. An additional source of data were the pre- and post-course student surveys designed by the instructors. Finally, the evaluators monitored the ENV 991 home page as a way of keeping current with assignments, discussions, and other course-related activities.

RESULTS

Just after the start of the semester, the instructors learned that the neighboring university does not accept pass/fail grades earned by its students while enrolled in courses outside the home institution. Rather than lose the three students from that university who were then enrolled in ENV 991 (one subsequently dropped the course), the instructors implemented a conventional grading system (A through C, and F) and applied it to all class members. This step provoked considerable disappointment among the students, some of whom indicated that it had changed the entire tenor of the course for them. Indeed, the shift in grading policy proved to be second only to a general dissatisfaction with the Web as the dominant negative finding of the evaluation. With respect to the Web, most students stated that (a) they often felt intimidated expressing their views in so public a forum, and (b) that they had to invest enormous amounts of time in performing the technical tasks required for making an informed posting on the Web site. The latter point also was mentioned by the instructors, who came to realize that they needed to be "on duty 24 hour hours a day" if they hoped to provide students with the prompt feedback that would make Web-based discourse more like a genuine conversation. In addition, students as well as instructors stated that the flexibility inherent in such a course allowed the students to approach their academic responsibilities somewhat more casually than in a conventional graduate course.

Given these complaints, it might seem that the course was viewed by the participants essentially as a failure. Such, however, was not the case. All participants described ENV 991 as a worthwhile undertaking and tended to regard their complaints as responses to start-up problems that could be remedied in the future. Students praised the course's interdisciplinary dimension and spoke highly of the interactions that took place during the in-person class sessions. In the words of one student, "The most I learned was when we were all together, hashing it out." From the instructors' standpoint, the semester's experience in ENV 991 provided an occasion for a fresh look at the types of student qualifications needed for a course of this type (such as enrolling doctoral rather than masters students) as well as for re-examining the technological tools available. For instance, the students' expressed desire for more real-time contact might be addressed through the incorporation of video technology.

IMPLICATIONS

ENV 991 offers some hints about what the future may hold for electronic applications to experiential education. Given the difficulties that were encountered by the students and instructors alike, electronic communications should probably be phased in gradually rather than initiated abruptly, and attention directed both to the technological skills required as well as the psychological acclimatization that some participants may need. One element of this process will be to prepare students adequately for the greater freedom and flexibility that they will experience in a Web-based course. Another issue will be to provide additional resources, perhaps in the form of part-time student assistants, to ease the burden that instructors may be faced with during their first few electronic courses.

Follow-Up Discussion to Case #4

Although small-scale evaluations, such as that described in this case, are often of interest only to the client (represented here by the instructors), the evaluation of ENV 991 was paid for by university-level decision makers. In what respects does this case study report direct attention to the broader issues involved? Shifting to a different issue, what are some of the potential ethical questions that an evaluator must confront in dealing with extremely small sample sizes? (Keep in mind that the enrollment for this course ranged only from five to six students over the semester.) Specify some of the steps that might be needed to preserve the confidentiality of responses under such circumstances.

Case #5
BRINGING THE WORKPLACE TO THE CLASSROOM: THE ENTREPRENEURS PROGRAM

Catherine E. Brawner and Thomas K. Miller, III
Research Triangle Educational Consultants and
North Carolina State University

Colleges and universities across the United States are facing growing demands to strengthen the experiential component of undergraduate education. Especially in preprofessional fields such as engineering, prospective employers are calling for more emphasis on the transmission of those skills that would allow graduates to become effective participants in all phases of workplace activity. One illustration of a new approach to engineering education can be found in the Entrepreneurs Program, sponsored by the Department of Electrical and Computer Engineering at North Carolina State University and by SUCCEED, a coalition of nine universities formed for the purpose of improving undergraduate education in engineering.

PROGRAM DESCRIPTION
The Entrepreneurs Program represents a blending of traditional and innovative instructional content and methods. Although primarily a course in engineering design, it also features a seminar series of speakers who focus on issues relevant to a start-up, high-tech enterprise (e.g., venture capitalists, successful and failed entrepreneurs, bankers, attorneys). The

purpose of the seminar series is to give students an understanding of all of the elements and challenges involved in starting a new company. The crux of the program, however, is the experiential component, in which students create companies around a theme and are led by seniors fulfilling their capstone design requirement. Each team has a faculty advisor and may also have an industry sponsor. There are no prerequisites for the course and undergraduate students may participate to the limits of their knowledge and expertise. They may also participate for multiple semesters. Unlike a traditional senior design course, seniors not only have the responsibility for the final product, but also for leading the team effectively. The theme of entrepreneurism came about as a result of the observation by the course designers that the nature of these project teams is not unlike that of a small start-up company developing a new product. Additionally, there is the expectation that small companies will be creating many new jobs for engineering graduates and that experience in this type of environment will prove beneficial in preparing graduates for the workplace.

The Evaluation

Due to SUCCEED's interest in developing course prototypes which can eventually be integrated into a university's engineering curriculum and exported to other universities, this evaluation was formative in nature. That is, it was done with the goal of providing feedback to the course instructor and funding sources on areas of success and areas for improvement. Therefore, the course was evaluated with respect to its own objectives, namely:

1. To retain student interest in engineering by involving them in meaningful design experiences early in their academic careers.
2. To improve the quality of the engineering design experience by involvement in multi-semester design activities.
3. To improve retention of underclassmen (freshmen and sophomores) by providing senior leaders as role models.
4. To improve teamwork skills by involving students in team-oriented projects, similar to what they will encounter in the workplace.
5. To improve leadership skills by assigning seniors management responsibilities for the project and team personnel.
6. To prepare students for the 21st-century workplace by exposing them to the dynamics of small, entrepreneurial companies.

Four methods of data collection were used to determine the degree to which these outcomes were being achieved: interviews with graduates who had taken the Entrepreneurs Program as their senior design course and with graduates who had a "regular" senior design experience; an electronic mail survey of all former participants who were still enrolled at NC State; an End-of-Course evaluation designed by the instructor and used over multiple semesters; and data collected regarding student retention from NC State's institutional research office. At the time of the evaluation, the course had been offered for six consecutive semesters.

RESULTS

In the six semesters that the Entrepreneurs Program had been offered, 159 students had participated. Of these, 113 had taken the class once and 46 had taken it more than once. With respect to retention, nearly all program participants remained at NC State, and those who began as engineers remained in engineering. A few of the students surveyed indicated that participation in the Entrepreneurs Program was one reason that they remained in engineering. Some students even transferred into engineering from other non-engineering majors after participating in the program. Similarly, the design experience appeared to have been positive, as the great majority of students who had taken other design and laboratory courses at NCSU rated the Entrepreneurs experience as superior to those. The multi-semester nature of the course does seem to have some appeal with most students saying that they would take the course again. Also, the senior leaders were judged to be somewhat effective, with two-thirds of the freshmen and sophomores stating that they had learned a lot from the seniors.

Students generally felt that their teamwork skills improved as a result of the program. This was especially true among the senior leaders. Other students were somewhat less likely to say that their teamwork skills had improved; in interviews and surveys, however, most of the freshmen and sophomores acknowledged the importance of working as a team and saw how they could apply teamwork skills in their jobs.

Senior leaders overwhelmingly felt that their leadership skills improved through their experience and some students chose the Entrepreneurs Program to fulfill their design requirement because of the leadership opportunity. Students who were not senior leaders were less positive about their leadership ability. Finally, the results generally suggested that students were well prepared for the work that they do after graduation or in cooperative education programs. Although most students do not go on to work for small entrepreneurial companies for their first jobs, they believe that the skills acquired or honed in the Entrepreneurs Program can be applied within larger companies. More generally, students indicated that they learned a lot about running a business from the seminar speakers and they enjoyed the business aspect of their work on their projects.

IMPLICATIONS

On balance, the strengths of the Entrepreneurs program far outweigh the weaknesses. This is reflected not only in regard to student retention, but also in the quality of the learning experience. In particular, students are encouraged to think for themselves, a refreshing change from cookbook labs and "one right answer." Yet it also seems safe to say that students get from the course in proportion to what they put into it. The freshmen and sophomores were found to have a wide range of experiences ranging from totally integrated into the team and working on an important component to being completely left out. Much of this variation can be attributed to personal commitment, but also to the presence or absence of friends and other support groups within the class. In addition, some thought should be given to the ways of insuring greater continuity of teams from semester to semester.

Follow-Up Discussion to Case #5

For purposes of this book, Case #5 has dealt primarily with the experiential component of the course and has done so chiefly through qualitative means. One intriguing possibility would be to extend the evaluation to include follow-up interviews with graduates, their co-workers, and employers. What sorts of questions might this extended evaluation address? What uses could be made of such data by the instructors and by other engineering educators? To what extent would it be feasible to apply a similar format to other experiential programs within your own undergraduate or secondary education curriculum?

REFERENCES

American Evaluation Association, Task Force on Guiding Principles for Evaluators. "Guiding Principles for Evaluators." *Guiding Principles for Evaluators.* Ed. W. R. Shadish, D. L. Newman, M. A. Scheirer, and C. Wye. San Francisco: Jossey-Bass, 1995. 19–26.

Campbell, D. T., and J. C. Stanley. *Experimental and Quasi-Experimental Designs for Research.* Chicago: Rand McNally, 1966.

Chamberlin, D., E. S. Chamberlin, N. E. Drought, and W. E. Scott. *Did They Succeed in College?* New York: Harper, 1942.

Close, J. C., and J. C. Impara, eds. *The Twelfth Mental Measurements Yearbook.* Lincoln, NE: Buros Institute/University of Nebraska Press, 1995.

Haller, E. J. "Cost Analysis for Educational Program Evaluation." *Evaluation in Education: Current Applications.* Ed. W. J. Popham. Berkeley: McCutchan, 1974. 401–450.

House, E. R. "Integrating the Quantitative and Qualitative." *The Qualitative-Quantitative Debate: New Perspectives.* Eds. C. S. Reichardt and S. F. Rallis. San Francisco: Jossey-Bass, 1994. 13–22.

Keller, G. *Academic Strategy: The Management Revolution in American Higher Education.* Baltimore: Johns Hopkins University Press, 1983.

Learned, W. S., and B. D. Wood. *The Student and His Knowledge.* New York: Carnegie Foundation for the Advancement of Teaching, 1938.

Madaus, G. F., M. Scriven, and D. L. Stufflebeam. *Evaluation Models: Viewpoints on Educational and Human Services Evaluation.* Boston: Kluwer-Nijhoff, 1983.

Popham, W. J. *Educational Evaluation.* 3rd ed. Boston: Allyn and Bacon, 1993.

Rossi, P. H. "The War between the Quals and the Quants: Is a Lasting Peace Possible?" *The Qualitative-Quantitative Debate: New Perspectives.* Ed. C. S. Reichardt and S. F. Rallis. San Francisco: Jossey-Bass, 1994. 23–36.

Sanders, J. R. *The Program Evaluation Standards.* Thousand Oaks, CA: Sage, 1994.

Scriven, M. "Pros and Cons about Goal-Free Evaluation." *Evaluation Comment* 3.4 (1972): 1–7.

Stake, R. E. "The Countenance of Educational Evaluation." *Teachers College Record* 68 (1967): 523–540.

Stufflebeam, D. L. "Introduction to the PDK Book *Educational Evaluation and Decision-Making.*" *Educational Evaluation: Theory and Practice.* Eds. B. R. Worthen and J. R. Sanders. Belmont CA: Wadsworth, 1973. 128–142.

Worthen, B. R., and J. R. Sanders. *Educational Evaluation: Alternative Approaches and Practical Guidelines.* New York: Longman, 1987.

Services and Publications of the National Society for Experiential Education

The National Society for Experiential Education is a nonprofit membership association and national resource center that promotes the use of learning through experience for:

- academic development
- civic and social responsibility
- career exploration
- cross-cultural awareness
- leadership development
- ethical development

NSEE's mission is to foster the effective use of experience as an integral part of education, in order to empower learners and promote the common good. Founded in 1971, NSEE assists schools, colleges, universities, and organizations in the field of experiential education, which includes:

- school-to-work
- service-learning
- internships
- field studies
- study abroad programs

- cooperative education
- leadership development programs
- practicum experiences
- active learning in the classroom

NSEE publishes the *NSEE Quarterly,* resource papers, monographs, and books, including:

- *Combining Service and Learning: A Resource Book for Community and Public Service*
- *Service-Learning Reader: Reflections and Perspectives on Service*
- *Research Agenda for Combining Service and Learning in the 1990s*
- *The National Directory of Internships*
- *The Experienced Hand: A Student Manual for Making the Most of an Internship*
- *The Internship as Partnership: A Handbook for Campus-Based Coordinators & Advisors*
- *The Internship as Partnership: A Handbook for Businesses, Nonprofits, and Government Agencies*
- *Strengthening Experiential Education within Your Institution*
- *Legal Issues in Experiential Education*
- *Origins and Implications of the AmeriCorps National Service Program* and other publications covering issues of Practice and Application, Rationale and Theory, and Research

NSEE's National Resource Center for Experiential and Service Learning provides information and referrals on the design and administration of experiential education programs, policy issues, research, and more. NSEE sponsors national and regional conferences and offers consulting services for those wishing to strengthen experiential education within their institution.

Benefits of NSEE membership include:

- a subscription to the *NSEE Quarterly—to keep you informed on innovations in the field*
- substantial discounts on publications, annual conference registration, consulting, and NSEE

Resource Center materials—*to give you the tools you need for improved practice*

- opportunities to join Special Interest Groups and Networks—*to connect you with colleagues across the country*
- opportunities to participate in special projects—*to test new experiential learning approaches*
- full voting privileges as well as eligibility for election or appointment to the NSEE Board of Directors—*to exercise leadership in the organization and the field*

For more information or to become a member, contact NSEE:

3509 Haworth Drive, Suite 207
Raleigh, NC 27609
919/787-3263
919/787-3381 fax
nsee@netstart.net
http://www.nsee.org